An inspirational book to help with the
journey of strength.

By Cara Barilla

"Sometimes revealing your inner most weakness can highlight your strengths to help you guide yourself through your journey. Don't be afraid to understand the depths of your hidden weaknesses & power to heal your spirit and to rise from your challenge."

"Evolving from your surroundings is inevitable. It is a gift from your higher self to move on. Release the toxic energy from your surroundings and watch your spirit reveal your true potential."

"Don't forget to step down, slow down and recognise what you need to do to make this situation easier. Knowing how much weight you should carry during this time is a true soul challenge."

"When you recharge your mind by slowing down your surroundings you will fuel your inner power and prepare yourself for life challenges to come."

"Close your eyes and breathe; As fast paced living may create more blockages than expected. Meditation and relaxation techniques calms your nerves and sends a healthy rhythm to your higher self."

"Once your surroundings are loved and cared for, your inner self will feel nurture. Create a sanctuary within your surroundings. Crystal placement, plants and de cluttering are great methods of nurturing your surroundings."

"Your loudest moments are when you are silent."

"Ask yourself what you truly need right now, what is important and what is insignificant. Your higher self truly knows what you can live with or without."

"The power of looking at yourself in the mirror with self-love and treating your body with self-harmony is forever bountiful and soul recharging."

"Your surroundings are your gifts to yourself. Subconsciously you've asked for your surroundings. Embrace what you have and receive the vibration of gratitude."

"Recharge your soul with fresh open windows. Natural daylight spreads harmonious natural energy and releases toxic energy from yourself and the home."

"The sun will forever amplify your inner self and let your soul shine. Recharge your crystals under the sun and feed your soul with sunlight to awaken your inner fire."

"Walking barefoot amid fresh damp earth creates electric energy through your energetic field. You are stronger than you feel, let your body ground yourself for clear thinking and fresh ideas."

"Using your power through passion is an emotionally rich life."

"Cleanse toxic energy and hydrate your soul with purified water. Being around water will allow you to release any built-up emotional tension and fill your spirit with clarity and inspiration."

"Find self-love through long air-filled walks. Bush walks, bay walks and beachside walks will allow fresh oxygen to fulfill your self-healing needs."

"When there is need for self-love, meditation to connect with your higher self or other dimensions is right at your command. Trust yourself and channel light and love."

"Time will always be your healer, helper and your hero."

"Now is your time to seek for help. Sometimes when you ask others you are in fact, asking yourself and recharging your core power."

"Make your own magic happen by exploding your inner most desires out into the universe. Your deliverance of unique ideas are more useful than you think."

"Look around, look inside and say "I love you". It is a true source of power when love and care is activated."

"Help yourself by helping others. Let your spirit shine full of light and bring angelic power to your surface."

"You are a sacred vessel with a touch that can not only change the lives of others, but can source healing power."

"Fuel your positive health with the power of aromatic fragrances through nature. Unlocking a piece of your soul through the power of scent is magical."

"Trust your inner angelic power and allow the sounds of purity to amplify over your sacred space. You can hear light and can channel the messages of purity. Nature sounds and the sounds of positive wisdom are strong sounds of purity.

"Take a deep breath, close your eyes and channel your higher self. Your inner source is guiding you the way to clarity. Trust your visions."

"Giving to those who are less fortunate is the same as giving to those who are fortunate; For we are all struggling in many different forms. Understand how different people may be at loss and try to give back."

"Don't be afraid to walk away. Remove yourself from a conversation if it doesn't serve you any good. Clear your energy from any negative surroundings if you feel it is taking away your power."

"The best way to generate power that is pure and potent is to become the light. The peacemaker within you knows when to choose your battles and stay humble."

"Recognition for the little things can help bring people out of the darkness. Words are very powerful. And especially your healing power. Your true tool is your voice."

"Learn that the best methods of harmonising silence can be when you least expect it and when it is out of your control. This is a powerful lesson."

"Give the power of time lots of love and appreciation by honouring your past, journaling into the future as a sacred path & staying in love with the gift of your present."

"You are a gift to yourself. From time to time stop and thank yourself & reward yourself with unconditional love. you have powerful self-healing powers."

"You are swimming in the bliss of life. Float in your inner gratitude and feel the depth of blessings which journeys under you each day."

"You are a beautiful song that needs to sing out the love that has been given to your soul.

"Continue to journal what you wish for; Your hopes and dreams in writing and your strong will power can catchup to your reality."

"A new journey lies ahead of you if you'll let it. It's time to open up your heart, release your inner passion and embark on a powerful soul adventure; For you have a story that you haven't written yet."

"Where does your power source come from? Be aware of when you are most empowered and happy. Do music, art, people, words, or anything else particularly recharge or drain you? Awareness is powerful."

"Asking for help is always a soul strength. When you surrender to the help of others you are witnessing true soul ascension to a higher vibration; For your ego ceases to repeat itself."

"Create a new piece of power within by keeping you next steps in this journey of life a mystery. When you hold your next steps within your mind and circulate your thoughts; manifestation will amplify."

"You are infinite energy."

"To search for life is to live; and to seek the meaning of creation is to create. You are made to create your own blueprint of life. Now is the time to create your path and live. Your inner power is ready to make magic. Let your soul create a masterpiece."

"Balancing many tasks can be possible at this time. Relax your mind and Harmonise your soul by adding small pieces of what you love to create a new routine of balance and change."

"Let your soul say no. Let the power of pausing, stepping back and realising that all you need to do is slow down and not surrender yourself to every door. Sometimes a boundary can be your most powerful wand of guidance."

"Harvest your power by the strength of resisting. Take time now to assess your souls need and guide your power to what you feel is right. Sometimes when you look at your path from a distance you can see your direction clearer."

"The essence of life comes from unconditional purity. Shine life through the beauty of purity and the power of light."

"Living in pure light is powerful; seeing beauty and light within the darkest of people, energies and circumstances can heal and bring out deep hidden light from yourself. when you have experienced living in pure darkness can also help you highlight the purity which your soul truly needs.

"Energies are moveable, whether given out or taken away. Surround yourself with people of light energies so you can always exchange and give out all the many forms of good energy. This soul exchange can recharge and heal different parts of your chakras & blockages."

"Within you is the power to create anything you desire. Hold your mind onto that power and that's where the energy will rest."

"Your energy within you has the ability to shift. You can channel the power you long for. Close your eyes and dream. Your thoughts will collect the energy it is attracting at that very moment."

"Rise above that negative energy and believe in who you want to be. Your inner power wants you to shine and live within your true souls potential. You are magical and powerful."

"Have inner belief in what you want. Your capabilities are limitless and you are an energy source of pure creation."

"When you think of something negative and is taking away your happiness, just ask your higher self to remove all negative thoughts that does not serve you. This is energetic power."

"Sometimes the most powerful people in the room aren't the loudest or extroverted."

"The power of moving energy around is possible as everything is energy. Once you walk yourself into a place of where you want to be whether it be a physical or mental place, you are instantly changing your frequency to your desire."

"Goals always help shift your power to its high potential. Write mini goals down to let your higher self know where you want to gravitate to. The power of frequencies will shift to you."

"Love is a strong source of energy. Once you give yourself and others pure love you will find a new way to recharge your power."

"Ignite your power again by de-cluttering your home; For your surroundings are a reflection of your mind."

"Once your surroundings are clear, you will have the ability to channel in higher vibrational power."

"Guiding others to their power is connecting to your purest power source."

"Power is useless when there is little hope. Love yourself and believe in your inner most powerful worth."

"Your power has its own voice. Even before you speak you have already flooded the room with your intentions."

"Never lower your energy or dim your flame to please others. Your subconscious doesn't know any different and will rest your power there."

"Being powerful is to know when to shed and share your power and when to protect yourself."

"Loving power expands energy; hateful power contracts your energy. When you love out to the world you are loving your inner power."

"When feeling stressed, exercise the power of shifting energy by moving around. This will circulate and recharge your pure energy."

"Loving your inner minds world is the power for creating your external world."

"Cultivating your uniqueness in all its depths is positively pure power."

"Being true to yourself is opening up your power source."

"Your mind today is a reflection of your physical tomorrow."

"Recharging your power is magical; Some find it through song, words, touch, colours, craft and scent."

"Helping others is God's natural power source."

"The power of imagery ignites the flame and warms the soul. Use positive visualisation to explore "your minds journey. It's okay to explore within. Give yourself the powerful gift of imagination to heal."

"Letting go of the ego is opening up a new power force."

"Those who have strong will are surrounded by their inner fire."

"Negative thoughts don't belong to you; once they come in you have to power to ask your higher self to remove them immediately."

"Faith is the most powerful source of energy you can hold in your heart and release with love."

"For those who have let you down and give you extra weight on your shoulders; you have the power to release them from your mind. Over-thoughts are just impractical memories. Feel the negative energy lift from your body the moment you connect with those who care for you. Embrace the warm exchange of kindness."

"Some people fear the fire;
Others will become it."

"Your thoughts are the seeds that you plant yourself. Be aware of what you sow."

"Your mind can either enslave or empower you; Give respect, love and cleanse. Then all will align."

"To be powerful is to be fearless."

"When you ignite your inner power, you have control of your destiny."

"When you change the way you look at your surroundings, your surroundings will change."

"It's always the small brushstrokes that will make your beautiful painting."

"You can see how much you really want something when your passion creeps up from your heart and gets caught in your mind."

"The best way to predict your future is to use your power and create it."

"Everything you desire is on the other side of fear. Release and create."

"Speaking your truth is breathing out your inner fire."

"Your inner power lives deep inside you.
Created by passion."

"When there's belief; You can channel your inner power anywhere, anytime."

"You cannot move on unless you give yourself permission to."

"Be present in every single circumstance like you deserve to be there."

"Our inner power is the key to the multi universe."

"Inner love shields your power. When you love yourself that's the moment when your heart releases power."

"Power lies in your neck to keep your chin up high, and in your heart to value your true existence."

"Allowing yourself to make mistakes along the way and to be wrong is true power."

"The power within you is accepting of all the energies; Energies that are compatible with you, and energies that are not."

"When you focus on your own passion and not others, that is true power."

"The divine pattern of life decided for you to be here on earth here and now. Value your precious soul and use your inner power to drive to your new adventure."

"Yes, there is darkness everywhere; But also focus that there is lightness everywhere too."

"The heart is the map to your passions destination. Your power is the legs that will walk you there."

"Your words contain energy. Words are soulfully powerful. Remember to always say kind words to yourself and others."

"Remember; finding perfection at sight does not exist. Being passionately in love with uniqueness is simply the feeling of perfection."

"When you walk through life with your passion through your eyes; you've already succeeded."

"Yes, you can be powerful, but are you powerful enough to help others when they are powerless?"

"Your power cannot be stopped. Ever. Allow your inner power to live on the surface and shine your hearts desires."

"Nobody can be you; Not even if they tried. When you value your uniqueness, you are in touch of your soul."

"Your potential is the galaxy."

"Remember that your minds power is infinite and magical."

"Life is a great way to get your soul to shine through the sun and live out what the source of power can truly create."

"Feeling lifeless at times is your natural way of telling you to recharge your soul."

"To lift up your power; is to learn where it's source stems from."

"Light brings us day; As belief brings us power."

"There will always be some pain; Your inner power strengthens with venerability."

"Inner power will always stand out in a foreign place. Don't be afraid to explore new unexplored territory."

"Feeling down is a way of being blessed with gratitude; When you feel darkness there is always light. you will travel fast towards the light and rise greater than ever before."

"If you ever feel that moment when someone may be intentionally hurting your feelings or taking away your energy just remember; they are trying to take away your full energy because they are running out."

"Be grateful that you have lived out those moments where you endured tough situations. Self-gratification is a strong power charge."

"You are a strong magnet to energy; Whether positive or negative. Be aware of the people you surround yourself with as this energy will creep up upon you."

"Close your eyes. This is your inner home, your place of creation; Open your eyes. These are your results of what you've previously manifested into your world whether it may be good or bad. The choice is yours to close your eyes and create in light or darkness. consciously or subconsciously."

"You are your own power source and nobody has the ability to control it without your consent."

"Which emotion do you feel you live & settle in from day-to-day. This helps you understand what frequency you naturally settle in."

"Sometimes when others take away your energy, they don't realise they are de-cluttering your mind and energy field for something greater."

"You are worthy. Don't ever let people try and question your worth or how hard you worked to be in the place you are in. You need to question why these people who question you are in your near surroundings."

"God bless you. These words are outstandingly powerful. You are blessed, guided and full of love and support, even if you don't see it!"

www.ingramcontent.com/pod-product-compliance
Lightning Source LLC
Chambersburg PA
CBHW060647150426
42811CB00086B/2452/J